MEMORIES

SPACE FOR A PICTURE OR SKETCH

NOTES

DATE: ____ / LOCATION: ____

WEATHER: ☐ HOT ☐ COLD ☐ MILD

TIME: ____ START ____ FINISH ____ TOTAL DURATION ____ BREAK

TOTAL DISTANCE: ____ TYPE: ____

ELEVATION GAIN/LOSS: ____

TRAIL TYPE: ____ OUT & BACK ____ LOOP ____ ONE WAY / SHUTTLE ____

THE HIKE ☆☆☆☆☆

TRAIL(S): ____

START LATITUDE/LONGITUDE: ____

MOBILE PHONE SIGNAL: ____ CARRIER: ____

TERRAIN: ____ ☐ FIRST VISIT ☐ RETURN VISIT

COMPANION(S): ____

FACILITIES: ____

OBSERVANCES: ____

TRAIL & WEATHER CONDITIONS: ____

BEVERAGES & FOOD, GEAR: ____

NOTES FOR THE NEXT TIME: ____

OVERALL RATING:

MEMORIES

SPACE FOR A PICTURE OR SKETCH

NOTES

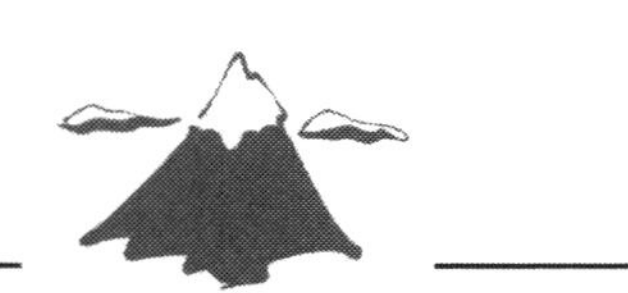

DATE: / LOCATION:

WEATHER: ☐ HOT ☐ COLD ☐ MILD

TIME:

START FINISH TOTAL DURATION BREAK

TOTAL DISTANCE: TYPE:

ELEVATION GAIN/LOSS:

TRAIL TYPE: OUT & BACK LOOP ONE WAY / SHUTTLE

THE HIKE ☆☆☆☆☆

TRAIL(S):

START LATITUDE/LONGITUDE:

MOBILE PHONE SIGNAL: CARRIER:

TERRAIN: ☐ FIRST VISIT ☐ RETURN VISIT

COMPANION(S):

FACILITIES:

OBSERVANCES:

TRAIL & WEATHER CONDITIONS:

BEVERAGES & FOOD, GEAR:

NOTES FOR THE NEXT TIME:

OVERALL RATING:

MEMORIES

SPACE FOR A PICTURE OR SKETCH

NOTES

DATE: / LOCATION:

WEATHER: ☐ HOT ☐ COLD ☐ MILD

TIME:

START FINISH TOTAL DURATION BREAK

TOTAL DISTANCE: TYPE:

ELEVATION GAIN/LOSS:

TRAIL TYPE: OUT & BACK LOOP ONE WAY / SHUTTLE

THE HIKE ☆☆☆☆☆

TRAIL(S):

START LATITUDE/LONGITUDE:

MOBILE PHONE SIGNAL: CARRIER:

TERRAIN: ☐ FIRST VISIT ☐ RETURN VISIT

COMPANION(S):

FACILITIES:

OBSERVANCES:

TRAIL & WEATHER CONDITIONS:

BEVERAGES & FOOD, GEAR:

NOTES FOR THE NEXT TIME:

OVERALL RATING:

MEMORIES

SPACE FOR A PICTURE OR SKETCH

NOTES

DATE: / LOCATION:

WEATHER: ☐ HOT ☐ COLD ☐ MILD

TIME:

START FINISH TOTAL DURATION BREAK

TOTAL DISTANCE: TYPE:

ELEVATION GAIN/LOSS:

TRAIL TYPE: OUT & BACK LOOP ONE WAY / SHUTTLE

THE HIKE ☆☆☆☆☆

TRAIL(S):

START LATITUDE/LONGITUDE:

MOBILE PHONE SIGNAL: CARRIER:

TERRAIN: ☐ FIRST VISIT ☐ RETURN VISIT

COMPANION(S):

FACILITIES:

OBSERVANCES:

TRAIL & WEATHER CONDITIONS:

BEVERAGES & FOOD, GEAR:

NOTES FOR THE NEXT TIME:

OVERALL RATING:

MEMORIES

SPACE FOR A PICTURE OR SKETCH

NOTES

DATE: / LOCATION:

WEATHER: ☐ HOT ☐ COLD ☐ MILD

TIME:

START FINISH TOTAL DURATION BREAK

TOTAL DISTANCE: TYPE:

ELEVATION GAIN/LOSS:

TRAIL TYPE: OUT & BACK LOOP ONE WAY / SHUTTLE

THE HIKE ☆☆☆☆☆

TRAIL(S):

START LATITUDE/LONGITUDE:

MOBILE PHONE SIGNAL: CARRIER:

TERRAIN: ☐ FIRST VISIT ☐ RETURN VISIT

COMPANION(S):

FACILITIES:

OBSERVANCES:

TRAIL & WEATHER CONDITIONS:

BEVERAGES & FOOD, GEAR:

NOTES FOR THE NEXT TIME:

OVERALL RATING:

MEMORIES

SPACE FOR A PICTURE OR SKETCH

NOTES

DATE: ______ / LOCATION: ______

WEATHER: ☐ HOT ☐ COLD ☐ MILD

TIME: ______ START ______ FINISH ______ TOTAL DURATION ______ BREAK

TOTAL DISTANCE: ______ TYPE: ______

ELEVATION GAIN/LOSS: ______

TRAIL TYPE: ______ OUT & BACK ______ LOOP ______ ONE WAY / SHUTTLE ______

THE HIKE ☆☆☆☆☆

TRAIL(S): ______

START LATITUDE/LONGITUDE: ______

MOBILE PHONE SIGNAL: ______ CARRIER: ______

TERRAIN: ______ ☐ FIRST VISIT ☐ RETURN VISIT

COMPANION(S): ______

FACILITIES: ______

OBSERVANCES: ______

TRAIL & WEATHER CONDITIONS: ______

BEVERAGES & FOOD, GEAR: ______

NOTES FOR THE NEXT TIME: ______

OVERALL RATING:

MEMORIES

SPACE FOR A PICTURE OR SKETCH

NOTES

DATE: ______ / LOCATION: ______

WEATHER: ☐ HOT ☐ COLD ☐ MILD

TIME: ______ ______ ______ ______

START FINISH TOTAL DURATION BREAK

TOTAL DISTANCE: ______ TYPE: ______

ELEVATION GAIN/LOSS: ______

TRAIL TYPE: ___ OUT & BACK ___ LOOP ___ ONE WAY / SHUTTLE ___

THE HIKE ☆☆☆☆☆

TRAIL(S): ______

______

START LATITUDE/LONGITUDE: ______

MOBILE PHONE SIGNAL: ______ CARRIER: ______

TERRAIN: ______ ☐ FIRST VISIT ☐ RETURN VISIT

COMPANION(S): ______

FACILITIES: ______

OBSERVANCES: ______

TRAIL & WEATHER CONDITIONS: ______

BEVERAGES & FOOD, GEAR: ______

NOTES FOR THE NEXT TIME: ______

______

OVERALL RATING:

MEMORIES

SPACE FOR A PICTURE OR SKETCH

NOTES

DATE: / LOCATION:

WEATHER: ☐ HOT ☐ COLD ☐ MILD

TIME:

START FINISH TOTAL DURATION BREAK

TOTAL DISTANCE: TYPE:

ELEVATION GAIN/LOSS:

TRAIL TYPE: OUT & BACK LOOP ONE WAY / SHUTTLE

THE HIKE ☆☆☆☆☆

TRAIL(S):

START LATITUDE/LONGITUDE:

MOBILE PHONE SIGNAL: CARRIER:

TERRAIN: ☐ FIRST VISIT ☐ RETURN VISIT

COMPANION(S):

FACILITIES:

OBSERVANCES:

TRAIL & WEATHER CONDITIONS:

BEVERAGES & FOOD, GEAR:

NOTES FOR THE NEXT TIME:

OVERALL RATING:

MEMORIES

SPACE FOR A PICTURE OR SKETCH

NOTES

DATE: / LOCATION:

WEATHER: ☐HOT ☐COLD ☐MILD

TIME:

START FINISH TOTAL DURATION BREAK

TOTAL DISTANCE: TYPE:

ELEVATION GAIN/LOSS:

TRAIL TYPE: OUT & BACK LOOP ONE WAY / SHUTTLE

THE HIKE ☆☆☆☆☆

TRAIL(S):

START LATITUDE/LONGITUDE:

MOBILE PHONE SIGNAL: CARRIER:

TERRAIN: ☐ FIRST VISIT ☐ RETURN VISIT

COMPANION(S):

FACILITIES:

OBSERVANCES:

TRAIL & WEATHER CONDITIONS:

BEVERAGES & FOOD, GEAR:

NOTES FOR THE NEXT TIME:

OVERALL RATING:

MEMORIES

SPACE FOR A PICTURE OR SKETCH

NOTES

DATE: / LOCATION:

WEATHER: ☐ HOT ☐ COLD ☐ MILD

TIME:

START FINISH TOTAL DURATION BREAK

TOTAL DISTANCE: TYPE:

ELEVATION GAIN/LOSS:

TRAIL TYPE: OUT & BACK LOOP ONE WAY / SHUTTLE

THE HIKE ☆☆☆☆☆

TRAIL(S):

START LATITUDE/LONGITUDE:

MOBILE PHONE SIGNAL: CARRIER:

TERRAIN: ☐ FIRST VISIT ☐ RETURN VISIT

COMPANION(S):

FACILITIES:

OBSERVANCES:

TRAIL & WEATHER CONDITIONS:

BEVERAGES & FOOD, GEAR:

NOTES FOR THE NEXT TIME:

OVERALL RATING:

MEMORIES

SPACE FOR A PICTURE OR SKETCH

NOTES

DATE: / LOCATION:

WEATHER: ☐ HOT ☐ COLD ☐ MILD

TIME:

START FINISH TOTAL DURATION BREAK

TOTAL DISTANCE: TYPE:

ELEVATION GAIN/LOSS:

TRAIL TYPE: OUT & BACK LOOP ONE WAY / SHUTTLE

THE HIKE ☆☆☆☆☆

TRAIL(S):

START LATITUDE/LONGITUDE:

MOBILE PHONE SIGNAL: CARRIER:

TERRAIN: ☐ FIRST VISIT ☐ RETURN VISIT

COMPANION(S):

FACILITIES:

OBSERVANCES:

TRAIL & WEATHER CONDITIONS:

BEVERAGES & FOOD, GEAR:

NOTES FOR THE NEXT TIME:

OVERALL RATING:

MEMORIES

SPACE FOR A PICTURE OR SKETCH

NOTES

DATE: / LOCATION:

WEATHER: ☐HOT ☐COLD ☐MILD

TIME:

START FINISH TOTAL DURATION BREAK

TOTAL DISTANCE: TYPE:

ELEVATION GAIN/LOSS:

TRAIL TYPE: OUT & BACK LOOP ONE WAY / SHUTTLE

THE HIKE ☆☆☆☆☆

TRAIL(S):

START LATITUDE/LONGITUDE:

MOBILE PHONE SIGNAL: CARRIER:

TERRAIN: ☐ FIRST VISIT ☐ RETURN VISIT

COMPANION(S):

FACILITIES:

OBSERVANCES:

TRAIL & WEATHER CONDITIONS:

BEVERAGES & FOOD, GEAR:

NOTES FOR THE NEXT TIME:

OVERALL RATING:

MEMORIES

SPACE FOR A PICTURE OR SKETCH

NOTES

DATE: ____ / LOCATION: ____

WEATHER: ☐ HOT ☐ COLD ☐ MILD

TIME: ____ ____ ____ ____
START FINISH TOTAL DURATION BREAK

TOTAL DISTANCE: ____ TYPE: ____

ELEVATION GAIN/LOSS: ____

TRAIL TYPE: ____ OUT & BACK ____ LOOP ____ ONE WAY / SHUTTLE ____

THE HIKE ☆☆☆☆☆

TRAIL(S): ____

START LATITUDE/LONGITUDE: ____

MOBILE PHONE SIGNAL: ____ CARRIER: ____

TERRAIN: ____ ☐ FIRST VISIT ☐ RETURN VISIT

COMPANION(S): ____

FACILITIES: ____

OBSERVANCES: ____

TRAIL & WEATHER CONDITIONS: ____

BEVERAGES & FOOD, GEAR: ____

NOTES FOR THE NEXT TIME: ____

OVERALL RATING: ____ ____ ____ ____ ____ ____

MEMORIES

SPACE FOR A PICTURE OR SKETCH

NOTES

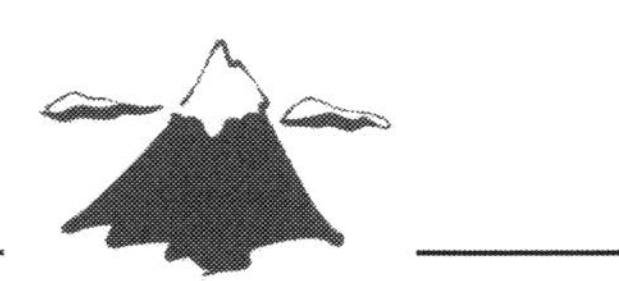

DATE: ______________ / LOCATION: ______________

WEATHER: ☐ HOT ☐ COLD ☐ MILD

TIME: ....
START FINISH TOTAL DURATION BREAK

TOTAL DISTANCE: ______________ TYPE: ______________

ELEVATION GAIN/LOSS: ______________

TRAIL TYPE: ____ OUT & BACK ____ LOOP ____ ONE WAY / SHUTTLE ____

THE HIKE ☆☆☆☆☆

TRAIL(S): ______________

____

START LATITUDE/LONGITUDE: ______________

MOBILE PHONE SIGNAL: ______________ CARRIER: ______________

TERRAIN: ______________ ☐ FIRST VISIT ☐ RETURN VISIT

COMPANION(S): ______________

FACILITIES: ______________

OBSERVANCES: ______________

TRAIL & WEATHER CONDITIONS: ______________

BEVERAGES & FOOD, GEAR: ______________

NOTES FOR THE NEXT TIME: ______________

____

OVERALL RATING:

MEMORIES

SPACE FOR A PICTURE OR SKETCH

NOTES

DATE: / LOCATION:

WEATHER: ☐ HOT ☐ COLD ☐ MILD

TIME:

START FINISH TOTAL DURATION BREAK

TOTAL DISTANCE: TYPE:

ELEVATION GAIN/LOSS:

TRAIL TYPE: OUT & BACK LOOP ONE WAY / SHUTTLE

THE HIKE ☆☆☆☆☆

TRAIL(S):

START LATITUDE/LONGITUDE:

MOBILE PHONE SIGNAL: CARRIER:

TERRAIN: ☐ FIRST VISIT ☐ RETURN VISIT

COMPANION(S):

FACILITIES:

OBSERVANCES:

TRAIL & WEATHER CONDITIONS:

BEVERAGES & FOOD, GEAR:

NOTES FOR THE NEXT TIME:

OVERALL RATING:

MEMORIES

SPACE FOR A PICTURE OR SKETCH

NOTES

DATE: ______ / LOCATION: ______

WEATHER: ☐ HOT ☐ COLD ☐ MILD

TIME: ______ ______ ______ ______
START FINISH TOTAL DURATION BREAK

TOTAL DISTANCE: ______ TYPE: ______

ELEVATION GAIN/LOSS: ______

TRAIL TYPE: ___ OUT & BACK ___ LOOP ___ ONE WAY / SHUTTLE ___

THE HIKE ☆☆☆☆☆

TRAIL(S): ______

______

START LATITUDE/LONGITUDE: ______

MOBILE PHONE SIGNAL: ______ CARRIER: ______

TERRAIN: ______ ☐ FIRST VISIT ☐ RETURN VISIT

COMPANION(S): ______

FACILITIES: ______

OBSERVANCES: ______

TRAIL & WEATHER CONDITIONS: ______

BEVERAGES & FOOD, GEAR: ______

NOTES FOR THE NEXT TIME: ______

______

OVERALL RATING: ______ ______ ______ ______ ______ ______

MEMORIES

SPACE FOR A PICTURE OR SKETCH

NOTES

DATE: ______ / LOCATION: ______

WEATHER: ☐ HOT ☐ COLD ☐ MILD

TIME: ______ ______ ______ ______
START FINISH TOTAL DURATION BREAK

TOTAL DISTANCE: ______ TYPE: ______

ELEVATION GAIN/LOSS: ______

TRAIL TYPE: ______ OUT & BACK ______ LOOP ______ ONE WAY / SHUTTLE ______

THE HIKE ☆☆☆☆☆

TRAIL(S): ______

______

START LATITUDE/LONGITUDE: ______

MOBILE PHONE SIGNAL: ______ CARRIER: ______

TERRAIN: ______ ☐ FIRST VISIT ☐ RETURN VISIT

COMPANION(S): ______

FACILITIES: ______

OBSERVANCES: ______

TRAIL & WEATHER CONDITIONS: ______

BEVERAGES & FOOD, GEAR: ______

NOTES FOR THE NEXT TIME: ______

______

OVERALL RATING:

MEMORIES

SPACE FOR A PICTURE OR SKETCH

NOTES

DATE: .... / LOCATION: ....

WEATHER: ☐ HOT ☐ COLD ☐ MILD

TIME: ....

START FINISH TOTAL DURATION BREAK

TOTAL DISTANCE: .... TYPE: ....

ELEVATION GAIN/LOSS: ....

TRAIL TYPE: ...... OUT & BACK ...... LOOP ...... ONE WAY / SHUTTLE ......

THE HIKE ☆☆☆☆☆

TRAIL(S): ....

....

START LATITUDE/LONGITUDE: ....

MOBILE PHONE SIGNAL: .... CARRIER: ....

TERRAIN: .... ☐ FIRST VISIT ☐ RETURN VISIT

COMPANION(S): ....

FACILITIES: ....

OBSERVANCES: ....

TRAIL & WEATHER CONDITIONS: ....

BEVERAGES & FOOD, GEAR: ....

NOTES FOR THE NEXT TIME: ....

....

OVERALL RATING:

MEMORIES

SPACE FOR A PICTURE OR SKETCH

NOTES

DATE: ____________ / LOCATION: ____________

WEATHER: ☐ HOT ☐ COLD ☐ MILD

TIME: ....

START FINISH TOTAL DURATION BREAK

TOTAL DISTANCE: ____________ TYPE: ____________

ELEVATION GAIN/LOSS: ____________

TRAIL TYPE: ____ OUT & BACK ____ LOOP ____ ONE WAY / SHUTTLE ____

THE HIKE ☆☆☆☆☆

TRAIL(S): ____________

____

START LATITUDE/LONGITUDE: ____________

MOBILE PHONE SIGNAL: ____________ CARRIER: ____________

TERRAIN: ____________ ☐ FIRST VISIT ☐ RETURN VISIT

COMPANION(S): ____________

FACILITIES: ____________

OBSERVANCES: ____________

TRAIL & WEATHER CONDITIONS: ____________

BEVERAGES & FOOD, GEAR: ____________

NOTES FOR THE NEXT TIME: ____________

____

OVERALL RATING:

MEMORIES

SPACE FOR A PICTURE OR SKETCH

NOTES

DATE: / LOCATION:

WEATHER: ☐ HOT ☐ COLD ☐ MILD

TIME:

START FINISH TOTAL DURATION BREAK

TOTAL DISTANCE: TYPE:

ELEVATION GAIN/LOSS:

TRAIL TYPE: OUT & BACK LOOP ONE WAY / SHUTTLE

THE HIKE ☆☆☆☆☆

TRAIL(S):

START LATITUDE/LONGITUDE:

MOBILE PHONE SIGNAL: CARRIER:

TERRAIN: ☐ FIRST VISIT ☐ RETURN VISIT

COMPANION(S):

FACILITIES:

OBSERVANCES:

TRAIL & WEATHER CONDITIONS:

BEVERAGES & FOOD, GEAR:

NOTES FOR THE NEXT TIME:

OVERALL RATING:

MEMORIES

SPACE FOR A PICTURE OR SKETCH

NOTES

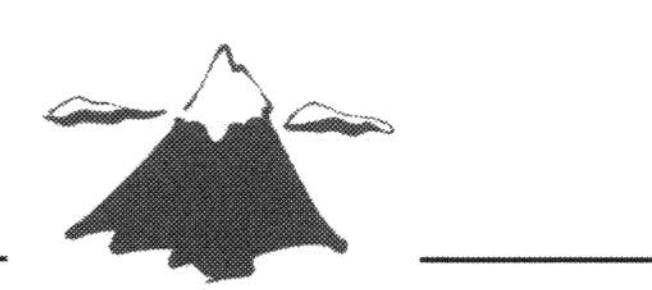

DATE: / LOCATION:

WEATHER: ☐HOT ☐COLD ☐MILD

TIME:

START FINISH TOTAL DURATION BREAK

TOTAL DISTANCE: TYPE:

ELEVATION GAIN/LOSS:

TRAIL TYPE: OUT & BACK LOOP ONE WAY / SHUTTLE

THE HIKE ☆☆☆☆☆

TRAIL(S):

START LATITUDE/LONGITUDE:

MOBILE PHONE SIGNAL: CARRIER:

TERRAIN: ☐ FIRST VISIT ☐ RETURN VISIT

COMPANION(S):

FACILITIES:

OBSERVANCES:

TRAIL & WEATHER CONDITIONS:

BEVERAGES & FOOD, GEAR:

NOTES FOR THE NEXT TIME:

OVERALL RATING:

MEMORIES

SPACE FOR A PICTURE OR SKETCH

NOTES

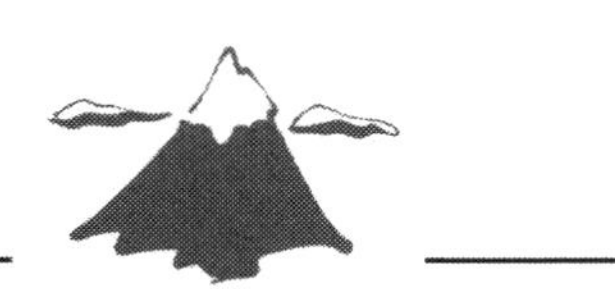

DATE: / LOCATION:

WEATHER: ☐ HOT ☐ COLD ☐ MILD

TIME:

START FINISH TOTAL DURATION BREAK

TOTAL DISTANCE: TYPE:

ELEVATION GAIN/LOSS:

TRAIL TYPE: OUT & BACK LOOP ONE WAY / SHUTTLE

THE HIKE ☆☆☆☆☆

TRAIL(S):

START LATITUDE/LONGITUDE:

MOBILE PHONE SIGNAL: CARRIER:

TERRAIN: ☐ FIRST VISIT ☐ RETURN VISIT

COMPANION(S):

FACILITIES:

OBSERVANCES:

TRAIL & WEATHER CONDITIONS:

BEVERAGES & FOOD, GEAR:

NOTES FOR THE NEXT TIME:

OVERALL RATING:

MEMORIES

SPACE FOR A PICTURE OR SKETCH

NOTES

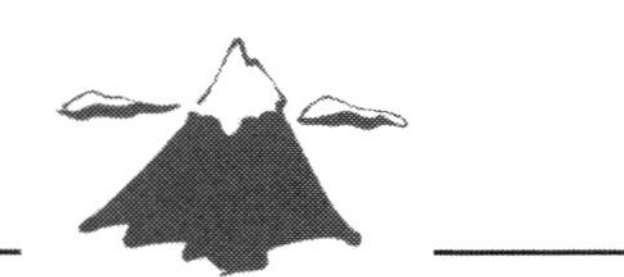

DATE: / LOCATION:

WEATHER: ☐ HOT ☐ COLD ☐ MILD

TIME:

START FINISH TOTAL DURATION BREAK

TOTAL DISTANCE: TYPE:

ELEVATION GAIN/LOSS:

TRAIL TYPE: OUT & BACK LOOP ONE WAY / SHUTTLE

THE HIKE

TRAIL(S):

START LATITUDE/LONGITUDE:

MOBILE PHONE SIGNAL: CARRIER:

TERRAIN: ☐ FIRST VISIT ☐ RETURN VISIT

COMPANION(S):

FACILITIES:

OBSERVANCES:

TRAIL & WEATHER CONDITIONS:

BEVERAGES & FOOD, GEAR:

NOTES FOR THE NEXT TIME:

OVERALL RATING:

MEMORIES

SPACE FOR A PICTURE OR SKETCH

NOTES

DATE: ______ / LOCATION: ______

WEATHER: ☐ HOT ☐ COLD ☐ MILD

TIME: ______ ______ ______ ______
START FINISH TOTAL DURATION BREAK

TOTAL DISTANCE: ______ TYPE: ______

ELEVATION GAIN/LOSS: ______

TRAIL TYPE: ______ OUT & BACK ______ LOOP ______ ONE WAY / SHUTTLE ______

THE HIKE ☆☆☆☆☆

TRAIL(S): ______

______

START LATITUDE/LONGITUDE: ______

MOBILE PHONE SIGNAL: ______ CARRIER: ______

TERRAIN: ______ ☐ FIRST VISIT ☐ RETURN VISIT

COMPANION(S): ______

FACILITIES: ______

OBSERVANCES: ______

TRAIL & WEATHER CONDITIONS: ______

BEVERAGES & FOOD, GEAR: ______

NOTES FOR THE NEXT TIME: ______

______

OVERALL RATING:

MEMORIES

SPACE FOR A PICTURE OR SKETCH

NOTES

DATE: ______ / LOCATION: ______

WEATHER: ☐ HOT ☐ COLD ☐ MILD

TIME: ______ START ______ FINISH ______ TOTAL DURATION ______ BREAK

TOTAL DISTANCE: ______ TYPE: ______

ELEVATION GAIN/LOSS: ______

TRAIL TYPE: ______ OUT & BACK ______ LOOP ______ ONE WAY / SHUTTLE ______

THE HIKE ☆☆☆☆☆

TRAIL(S): ______

START LATITUDE/LONGITUDE: ______

MOBILE PHONE SIGNAL: ______ CARRIER: ______

TERRAIN: ______ ☐ FIRST VISIT ☐ RETURN VISIT

COMPANION(S): ______

FACILITIES: ______

OBSERVANCES: ______

TRAIL & WEATHER CONDITIONS: ______

BEVERAGES & FOOD, GEAR: ______

NOTES FOR THE NEXT TIME: ______

OVERALL RATING:

MEMORIES

SPACE FOR A PICTURE OR SKETCH

NOTES

DATE: .... / LOCATION: ....

WEATHER: ☐ HOT ☐ COLD ☐ MILD

TIME: ....
START FINISH TOTAL DURATION BREAK

TOTAL DISTANCE: .... TYPE: ....

ELEVATION GAIN/LOSS: ....

TRAIL TYPE: ...... OUT & BACK ...... LOOP ...... ONE WAY / SHUTTLE ......

THE HIKE ☆☆☆☆☆

TRAIL(S): ....

....

START LATITUDE/LONGITUDE: ....

MOBILE PHONE SIGNAL: .... CARRIER: ....

TERRAIN: .... ☐ FIRST VISIT ☐ RETURN VISIT

COMPANION(S): ....

FACILITIES: ....

OBSERVANCES: ....

TRAIL & WEATHER CONDITIONS: ....

BEVERAGES & FOOD, GEAR: ....

NOTES FOR THE NEXT TIME: ....

....

OVERALL RATING:

MEMORIES

SPACE FOR A PICTURE OR SKETCH

NOTES

DATE: ____________ / LOCATION: ____________

WEATHER: ☐ HOT ☐ COLD ☐ MILD

TIME: ....
START FINISH TOTAL DURATION BREAK

TOTAL DISTANCE: ____________ TYPE: ____________

ELEVATION GAIN/LOSS: ____________

TRAIL TYPE: ____ OUT & BACK ____ LOOP ____ ONE WAY / SHUTTLE ____

THE HIKE ☆☆☆☆☆

TRAIL(S): ____________

START LATITUDE/LONGITUDE: ____________

MOBILE PHONE SIGNAL: ____________ CARRIER: ____________

TERRAIN: ____________ ☐ FIRST VISIT ☐ RETURN VISIT

COMPANION(S): ____________

FACILITIES: ____________

OBSERVANCES: ____________

TRAIL & WEATHER CONDITIONS: ____________

BEVERAGES & FOOD, GEAR: ____________

NOTES FOR THE NEXT TIME: ____________

OVERALL RATING:

MEMORIES

SPACE FOR A PICTURE OR SKETCH

NOTES

DATE: ______ / LOCATION: ______

WEATHER: ☐ HOT ☐ COLD ☐ MILD

TIME: ______ START ______ FINISH ______ TOTAL DURATION ______ BREAK

TOTAL DISTANCE: ______ TYPE: ______

ELEVATION GAIN/LOSS: ______

TRAIL TYPE: ______ OUT & BACK ______ LOOP ______ ONE WAY / SHUTTLE ______

THE HIKE ☆☆☆☆☆

TRAIL(S): ______

______

START LATITUDE/LONGITUDE: ______

MOBILE PHONE SIGNAL: ______ CARRIER: ______

TERRAIN: ______ ☐ FIRST VISIT ☐ RETURN VISIT

COMPANION(S): ______

FACILITIES: ______

OBSERVANCES: ______

TRAIL & WEATHER CONDITIONS: ______

BEVERAGES & FOOD, GEAR: ______

NOTES FOR THE NEXT TIME: ______

______

OVERALL RATING: ______ ______ ______ ______ ______ ______

MEMORIES

SPACE FOR A PICTURE OR SKETCH

NOTES

DATE: / LOCATION:

WEATHER: ☐ HOT ☐ COLD ☐ MILD

TIME:

START FINISH TOTAL DURATION BREAK

TOTAL DISTANCE: TYPE:

ELEVATION GAIN/LOSS:

TRAIL TYPE: OUT & BACK LOOP ONE WAY / SHUTTLE

THE HIKE ☆☆☆☆☆

TRAIL(S):

START LATITUDE/LONGITUDE:

MOBILE PHONE SIGNAL: CARRIER:

TERRAIN: ☐ FIRST VISIT ☐ RETURN VISIT

COMPANION(S):

FACILITIES:

OBSERVANCES:

TRAIL & WEATHER CONDITIONS:

BEVERAGES & FOOD, GEAR:

NOTES FOR THE NEXT TIME:

OVERALL RATING:

MEMORIES

SPACE FOR A PICTURE OR SKETCH

NOTES

DATE: ____ / LOCATION: ____

WEATHER: ☐ HOT ☐ COLD ☐ MILD

TIME: ____ ____ ____ ____
START FINISH TOTAL DURATION BREAK

TOTAL DISTANCE: ____ TYPE: ____

ELEVATION GAIN/LOSS: ____

TRAIL TYPE: ____ OUT & BACK ____ LOOP ____ ONE WAY / SHUTTLE ____

THE HIKE ☆☆☆☆☆

TRAIL(S): ____

START LATITUDE/LONGITUDE: ____
MOBILE PHONE SIGNAL: ____ CARRIER: ____

TERRAIN: ____ ☐ FIRST VISIT ☐ RETURN VISIT

COMPANION(S): ____

FACILITIES: ____

OBSERVANCES: ____

TRAIL & WEATHER CONDITIONS: ____

BEVERAGES & FOOD, GEAR: ____

NOTES FOR THE NEXT TIME: ____

OVERALL RATING:

MEMORIES

SPACE FOR A PICTURE OR SKETCH

NOTES

DATE: / LOCATION:

WEATHER: ☐ HOT ☐ COLD ☐ MILD

TIME:

START FINISH TOTAL DURATION BREAK

TOTAL DISTANCE: TYPE:

ELEVATION GAIN/LOSS:

TRAIL TYPE: OUT & BACK LOOP ONE WAY / SHUTTLE

THE HIKE ☆☆☆☆☆

TRAIL(S):

START LATITUDE/LONGITUDE:

MOBILE PHONE SIGNAL: CARRIER:

TERRAIN: ☐ FIRST VISIT ☐ RETURN VISIT

COMPANION(S):

FACILITIES:

OBSERVANCES:

TRAIL & WEATHER CONDITIONS:

BEVERAGES & FOOD, GEAR:

NOTES FOR THE NEXT TIME:

OVERALL RATING:

MEMORIES

SPACE FOR A PICTURE OR SKETCH

NOTES

DATE: / LOCATION:

WEATHER: ☐ HOT ☐ COLD ☐ MILD

TIME:

START FINISH TOTAL DURATION BREAK

TOTAL DISTANCE: TYPE:

ELEVATION GAIN/LOSS:

TRAIL TYPE: OUT & BACK LOOP ONE WAY / SHUTTLE

THE HIKE ☆☆☆☆☆

TRAIL(S):

START LATITUDE/LONGITUDE:

MOBILE PHONE SIGNAL: CARRIER:

TERRAIN: ☐ FIRST VISIT ☐ RETURN VISIT

COMPANION(S):

FACILITIES:

OBSERVANCES:

TRAIL & WEATHER CONDITIONS:

BEVERAGES & FOOD, GEAR:

NOTES FOR THE NEXT TIME:

OVERALL RATING:

MEMORIES

SPACE FOR A PICTURE OR SKETCH

NOTES

DATE: .... / LOCATION: ....

WEATHER: ☐ HOT ☐ COLD ☐ MILD

TIME: ....
START FINISH TOTAL DURATION BREAK

TOTAL DISTANCE: .... TYPE: ....

ELEVATION GAIN/LOSS: ....

TRAIL TYPE: .... OUT & BACK .... LOOP .... ONE WAY / SHUTTLE ....

THE HIKE ☆☆☆☆☆

TRAIL(S): ....

....

START LATITUDE/LONGITUDE: ....

MOBILE PHONE SIGNAL: .... CARRIER: ....

TERRAIN: .... ☐ FIRST VISIT ☐ RETURN VISIT

COMPANION(S): ....

FACILITIES: ....

OBSERVANCES: ....

TRAIL & WEATHER CONDITIONS: ....

BEVERAGES & FOOD, GEAR: ....

NOTES FOR THE NEXT TIME: ....

....

OVERALL RATING:

MEMORIES

SPACE FOR A PICTURE OR SKETCH

NOTES

DATE: / LOCATION:

WEATHER: ☐HOT ☐COLD ☐MILD

TIME:

START FINISH TOTAL DURATION BREAK

TOTAL DISTANCE: TYPE:

ELEVATION GAIN/LOSS:

TRAIL TYPE: OUT & BACK LOOP ONE WAY / SHUTTLE

THE HIKE ☆☆☆☆☆

TRAIL(S):

START LATITUDE/LONGITUDE:

MOBILE PHONE SIGNAL: CARRIER:

TERRAIN: ☐ FIRST VISIT ☐ RETURN VISIT

COMPANION(S):

FACILITIES:

OBSERVANCES:

TRAIL & WEATHER CONDITIONS:

BEVERAGES & FOOD, GEAR:

NOTES FOR THE NEXT TIME:

OVERALL RATING:

MEMORIES

SPACE FOR A PICTURE OR SKETCH

NOTES

DATE: / LOCATION:

WEATHER: ☐ HOT ☐ COLD ☐ MILD

TIME:

START FINISH TOTAL DURATION BREAK

TOTAL DISTANCE: TYPE:

ELEVATION GAIN/LOSS:

TRAIL TYPE: OUT & BACK LOOP ONE WAY / SHUTTLE

THE HIKE ☆☆☆☆☆

TRAIL(S):

START LATITUDE/LONGITUDE:

MOBILE PHONE SIGNAL: CARRIER:

TERRAIN: ☐ FIRST VISIT ☐ RETURN VISIT

COMPANION(S):

FACILITIES:

OBSERVANCES:

TRAIL & WEATHER CONDITIONS:

BEVERAGES & FOOD, GEAR:

NOTES FOR THE NEXT TIME:

OVERALL RATING:

MEMORIES

SPACE FOR A PICTURE OR SKETCH

NOTES

DATE: ____ / LOCATION: ____

WEATHER: ☐HOT ☐COLD ☐MILD

TIME: ____ START ____ FINISH ____ TOTAL DURATION ____ BREAK

TOTAL DISTANCE: ____ TYPE: ____

ELEVATION GAIN/LOSS: ____

TRAIL TYPE: ____ OUT & BACK ____ LOOP ____ ONE WAY / SHUTTLE ____

THE HIKE ☆☆☆☆☆

TRAIL(S): ____

START LATITUDE/LONGITUDE: ____

MOBILE PHONE SIGNAL: ____ CARRIER: ____

TERRAIN: ____ ☐ FIRST VISIT ☐ RETURN VISIT

COMPANION(S): ____

FACILITIES: ____

OBSERVANCES: ____

TRAIL & WEATHER CONDITIONS: ____

BEVERAGES & FOOD, GEAR: ____

NOTES FOR THE NEXT TIME: ____

OVERALL RATING:

MEMORIES

SPACE FOR A PICTURE OR SKETCH

NOTES

DATE: / LOCATION:

WEATHER: ☐ HOT ☐ COLD ☐ MILD

TIME:

START FINISH TOTAL DURATION BREAK

TOTAL DISTANCE: TYPE:

ELEVATION GAIN/LOSS:

TRAIL TYPE: OUT & BACK LOOP ONE WAY / SHUTTLE

THE HIKE ☆☆☆☆☆

TRAIL(S):

START LATITUDE/LONGITUDE:

MOBILE PHONE SIGNAL: CARRIER:

TERRAIN: ☐ FIRST VISIT ☐ RETURN VISIT

COMPANION(S):

FACILITIES:

OBSERVANCES:

TRAIL & WEATHER CONDITIONS:

BEVERAGES & FOOD, GEAR:

NOTES FOR THE NEXT TIME:

OVERALL RATING:

MEMORIES

SPACE FOR A PICTURE OR SKETCH

NOTES

DATE: ________ / LOCATION: ________

WEATHER: ☐ HOT ☐ COLD ☐ MILD

TIME: ________ ________ ________ ________
START FINISH TOTAL DURATION BREAK

TOTAL DISTANCE: ________ TYPE: ________

ELEVATION GAIN/LOSS: ________

TRAIL TYPE: ____ OUT & BACK ____ LOOP ____ ONE WAY / SHUTTLE ____

THE HIKE ☆☆☆☆☆

TRAIL(S): ________

____

START LATITUDE/LONGITUDE: ________

MOBILE PHONE SIGNAL: ________ CARRIER: ________

TERRAIN: ________ ☐ FIRST VISIT ☐ RETURN VISIT

COMPANION(S): ________

FACILITIES: ________

OBSERVANCES: ________

TRAIL & WEATHER CONDITIONS: ________

BEVERAGES & FOOD, GEAR: ________

NOTES FOR THE NEXT TIME: ________

____

OVERALL RATING:

MEMORIES

SPACE FOR A PICTURE OR SKETCH

NOTES

DATE: / LOCATION:

WEATHER: ☐ HOT ☐ COLD ☐ MILD

TIME:
START FINISH TOTAL DURATION BREAK

TOTAL DISTANCE: TYPE:

ELEVATION GAIN/LOSS:

TRAIL TYPE: OUT & BACK LOOP ONE WAY / SHUTTLE

THE HIKE ☆☆☆☆☆

TRAIL(S):

START LATITUDE/LONGITUDE:

MOBILE PHONE SIGNAL: CARRIER:

TERRAIN: ☐ FIRST VISIT ☐ RETURN VISIT

COMPANION(S):

FACILITIES:

OBSERVANCES:

TRAIL & WEATHER CONDITIONS:

BEVERAGES & FOOD, GEAR:

NOTES FOR THE NEXT TIME:

OVERALL RATING:

MEMORIES

SPACE FOR A PICTURE OR SKETCH

NOTES

DATE: ____ / LOCATION: ____

WEATHER: ☐ HOT ☐ COLD ☐ MILD

TIME: ____ ____ ____ ____
START FINISH TOTAL DURATION BREAK

TOTAL DISTANCE: ____ TYPE: ____

ELEVATION GAIN/LOSS: ____

TRAIL TYPE: ____ OUT & BACK ____ LOOP ____ ONE WAY / SHUTTLE ____

THE HIKE ☆☆☆☆☆

TRAIL(S): ____

____

START LATITUDE/LONGITUDE: ____

MOBILE PHONE SIGNAL: ____ CARRIER: ____

TERRAIN: ____ ☐ FIRST VISIT ☐ RETURN VISIT

COMPANION(S): ____

FACILITIES: ____

OBSERVANCES: ____

TRAIL & WEATHER CONDITIONS: ____

BEVERAGES & FOOD, GEAR: ____

NOTES FOR THE NEXT TIME: ____

____

OVERALL RATING:

MEMORIES

SPACE FOR A PICTURE OR SKETCH

NOTES

DATE: ______________ / LOCATION: ______________

WEATHER: ☐ HOT ☐ COLD ☐ MILD

TIME: ______ ______ ______ ______

START FINISH TOTAL DURATION BREAK

TOTAL DISTANCE: ______________ TYPE: ______________

ELEVATION GAIN/LOSS: ______________

TRAIL TYPE: ____ OUT & BACK ____ LOOP ____ ONE WAY / SHUTTLE ____

THE HIKE ☆☆☆☆☆

TRAIL(S): ______________

____

START LATITUDE/LONGITUDE: ______________

MOBILE PHONE SIGNAL: ______________ CARRIER: ______________

TERRAIN: ______________ ☐ FIRST VISIT ☐ RETURN VISIT

COMPANION(S): ______________

FACILITIES: ______________

OBSERVANCES: ______________

TRAIL & WEATHER CONDITIONS: ______________

BEVERAGES & FOOD, GEAR: ______________

NOTES FOR THE NEXT TIME: ______________

____

OVERALL RATING:

MEMORIES

SPACE FOR A PICTURE OR SKETCH

NOTES

DATE: .... / LOCATION: ....

WEATHER: ☐ HOT ☐ COLD ☐ MILD

TIME: ....

START FINISH TOTAL DURATION BREAK

TOTAL DISTANCE: .... TYPE: ....

ELEVATION GAIN/LOSS: ....

TRAIL TYPE: ...... OUT & BACK ...... LOOP ...... ONE WAY / SHUTTLE ......

THE HIKE ☆☆☆☆☆

TRAIL(S): ....

....

START LATITUDE/LONGITUDE: ....

MOBILE PHONE SIGNAL: .... CARRIER: ....

TERRAIN: .... ☐ FIRST VISIT ☐ RETURN VISIT

COMPANION(S): ....

FACILITIES: ....

OBSERVANCES: ....

TRAIL & WEATHER CONDITIONS: ....

BEVERAGES & FOOD, GEAR: ....

NOTES FOR THE NEXT TIME: ....

....

OVERALL RATING:

MEMORIES

SPACE FOR A PICTURE OR SKETCH

NOTES

DATE: / LOCATION:

WEATHER: ☐ HOT ☐ COLD ☐ MILD

TIME:

START FINISH TOTAL DURATION BREAK

TOTAL DISTANCE: TYPE:

ELEVATION GAIN/LOSS:

TRAIL TYPE: OUT & BACK LOOP ONE WAY / SHUTTLE

THE HIKE ☆☆☆☆☆

TRAIL(S):

START LATITUDE/LONGITUDE:

MOBILE PHONE SIGNAL: CARRIER:

TERRAIN: ☐ FIRST VISIT ☐ RETURN VISIT

COMPANION(S):

FACILITIES:

OBSERVANCES:

TRAIL & WEATHER CONDITIONS:

BEVERAGES & FOOD, GEAR:

NOTES FOR THE NEXT TIME:

OVERALL RATING:

MEMORIES

SPACE FOR A PICTURE OR SKETCH

NOTES

DATE: / LOCATION:

WEATHER: ☐ HOT ☐ COLD ☐ MILD

TIME:

START FINISH TOTAL DURATION BREAK

TOTAL DISTANCE: TYPE:

ELEVATION GAIN/LOSS:

TRAIL TYPE: OUT & BACK LOOP ONE WAY / SHUTTLE

THE HIKE ☆☆☆☆☆

TRAIL(S):

START LATITUDE/LONGITUDE:

MOBILE PHONE SIGNAL: CARRIER:

TERRAIN: ☐ FIRST VISIT ☐ RETURN VISIT

COMPANION(S):

FACILITIES:

OBSERVANCES:

TRAIL & WEATHER CONDITIONS:

BEVERAGES & FOOD, GEAR:

NOTES FOR THE NEXT TIME:

OVERALL RATING:

MEMORIES

SPACE FOR A PICTURE OR SKETCH

NOTES

DATE: ____________ / LOCATION: ____________

WEATHER: ☐ HOT ☐ COLD ☐ MILD

TIME: ____________ ____________ ____________ ____________

START FINISH TOTAL DURATION BREAK

TOTAL DISTANCE: ____________ TYPE: ____________

ELEVATION GAIN/LOSS: ____________

TRAIL TYPE: ______ OUT & BACK ______ LOOP ______ ONE WAY / SHUTTLE ______

THE HIKE ☆☆☆☆☆

TRAIL(S): ____________

____

START LATITUDE/LONGITUDE: ____________

MOBILE PHONE SIGNAL: ____________ CARRIER: ____________

TERRAIN: ____________ ☐ FIRST VISIT ☐ RETURN VISIT

COMPANION(S): ____________

FACILITIES: ____________

OBSERVANCES: ____________

TRAIL & WEATHER CONDITIONS: ____________

BEVERAGES & FOOD, GEAR: ____________

NOTES FOR THE NEXT TIME: ____________

____

OVERALL RATING: ______ ______ ______ ______ ______ ______

MEMORIES

SPACE FOR A PICTURE OR SKETCH

NOTES

DATE: / LOCATION:

WEATHER: ☐ HOT ☐ COLD ☐ MILD

TIME:

START FINISH TOTAL DURATION BREAK

TOTAL DISTANCE: TYPE:

ELEVATION GAIN/LOSS:

TRAIL TYPE: OUT & BACK LOOP ONE WAY / SHUTTLE

THE HIKE ☆☆☆☆☆

TRAIL(S):

START LATITUDE/LONGITUDE:

MOBILE PHONE SIGNAL: CARRIER:

TERRAIN: ☐ FIRST VISIT ☐ RETURN VISIT

COMPANION(S):

FACILITIES:

OBSERVANCES:

TRAIL & WEATHER CONDITIONS:

BEVERAGES & FOOD, GEAR:

NOTES FOR THE NEXT TIME:

OVERALL RATING:

MEMORIES

SPACE FOR A PICTURE OR SKETCH

NOTES

DATE: ______ / LOCATION: ______

WEATHER: ☐ HOT ☐ COLD ☐ MILD

TIME: ______ START ______ FINISH ______ TOTAL DURATION ______ BREAK

TOTAL DISTANCE: ______ TYPE: ______

ELEVATION GAIN/LOSS: ______

TRAIL TYPE: ______ OUT & BACK ______ LOOP ______ ONE WAY / SHUTTLE ______

THE HIKE ☆☆☆☆☆

TRAIL(S): ______

START LATITUDE/LONGITUDE: ______

MOBILE PHONE SIGNAL: ______ CARRIER: ______

TERRAIN: ______ ☐ FIRST VISIT ☐ RETURN VISIT

COMPANION(S): ______

FACILITIES: ______

OBSERVANCES: ______

TRAIL & WEATHER CONDITIONS: ______

BEVERAGES & FOOD, GEAR: ______

NOTES FOR THE NEXT TIME: ______

OVERALL RATING:

MEMORIES

SPACE FOR A PICTURE OR SKETCH

NOTES

DATE: ____________ / LOCATION: ____________

WEATHER: ☐ HOT ☐ COLD ☐ MILD

TIME: ....
START FINISH TOTAL DURATION BREAK

TOTAL DISTANCE: ____________ TYPE: ____________

ELEVATION GAIN/LOSS: ____________

TRAIL TYPE: ____ OUT & BACK ____ LOOP ____ ONE WAY / SHUTTLE ____

THE HIKE ☆☆☆☆☆

TRAIL(S): ____________

START LATITUDE/LONGITUDE: ____________

MOBILE PHONE SIGNAL: ____________ CARRIER: ____________

TERRAIN: ____________ ☐ FIRST VISIT ☐ RETURN VISIT

COMPANION(S): ____________

FACILITIES: ____________

OBSERVANCES: ____________

TRAIL & WEATHER CONDITIONS: ____________

BEVERAGES & FOOD, GEAR: ____________

NOTES FOR THE NEXT TIME: ____________

OVERALL RATING:

MEMORIES

SPACE FOR A PICTURE OR SKETCH

NOTES

Manufactured by Amazon.ca
Bolton, ON